EARLY ADVANCED

A Mighty Fortress Is Our

Hymn Arrangements for Solo Piano

Arranged by
Marilynn Ham

A companion CD is also available from FJH Music. This recording, CD1032, features Marilynn Ham performing all of the arrangements in this book.

Production: Frank and Gail Hackinson
Production Coordinator: Derek Richard
Editors: Lyndell Leatherman, Edwin McLean, and Yamilka Silvestrini
Cover: Keith Alexander
Engraving: Tempo Music Press, Inc.
Printer: Tempo Music Press, Inc.

THE
F·J·H
MUSIC
COMPANY
INC.

ISBN 1-56939-324-9

A Note from the Editor

I was privileged to be the editor on duty when Marilynn Ham entered the publishing scene back in 1985. At the time, she and her husband Robert were teaching at a church-related college on the windswept plains of Kansas. With a fair amount of fear and trepidation, she handed those initial manuscripts to a bookstore owner, who passed them along to a sales rep, who in turn passed them on to me.

Immediately I sensed that her arrangements demonstrated an anointing that went far beyond their impeccable theory, form, and technique, important as those components are. I was struck by her sensitivity to the messages of the lyrics associated with the tunes. It was as if she had been immersed in the truths of the hymns for so long that they had permeated her creative spirit. And so came into being the first of many piano solo books and recordings from Mrs. Ham.

As our professional and spiritual journeys have often intersected in the ensuing years, I have come to appreciate more and more Marilynn's grace and poise. I have watched as her profound confidence in her Creator has carried her through very deep waters. Her concerts are more than just skillful performances: they are testimonials from a woman who is totally devoted to her faith, family, and music.

And so it is a personal privilege and joy to present her latest volume of hymn settings for piano: *A Mighty Fortress Is Our God*. I believe that this will prove to be a valuable source of preludes, offertories, and postludes, as well as contest and recital material. Overall, these 10 arrangements have that vintage Marilynn Ham feel that church pianists nationwide have come to love and expect. But in addition, there is a surprise around every corner—from the Ferrante and Teicher-like cascading triads in *On Eagle's Wings* to the rollicking $\frac{6}{8}$ section in *Rejoice, Ye Pure in Heart*. In my mind's ear, I can hear pianists everywhere rising up and calling Marilynn blessed as they prepare these pieces. And to that I will add a hearty "amen!"

Lyndell Leatherman

Marilynn Ham

Pianist Marilynn Ham has captivated audiences around the country with her solo performances. Greatly influenced by church music as a child, Marilynn, the oldest of 15 siblings, accompanied her family, playing arrangements by ear when she was in high school. She went on to earn bachelor's and master's degrees in piano performance from Northern Michigan University and the University of Wisconsin–Madison, respectively. While at NMU, she was honored with the Most Outstanding Music Student award.

Previously, Mrs. Ham taught for 10 years at Barclay College in Haviland, Kansas, where she was honored as Professor of the Year in 1981 and again in 1987. Currently artist-in-residence and professor of music at Bethel College in Mishawaka, Indiana, Marilynn teaches applied piano, utilizing sacred and classical repertoire. In addition, she is in constant demand as an arranger, recording artist, and clinician.

Marilynn and her husband Robert reside in Mishawaka, where Bob serves at Bethel College as choir director and chairman of the Fine Arts Division. They have two children, Norris and Meryl.

Contents

A Mighty Fortress Is Our God

Ein' Feste Burg

Martin Luther
Arranged by Marilynn Ham

6

A little slower, confidently

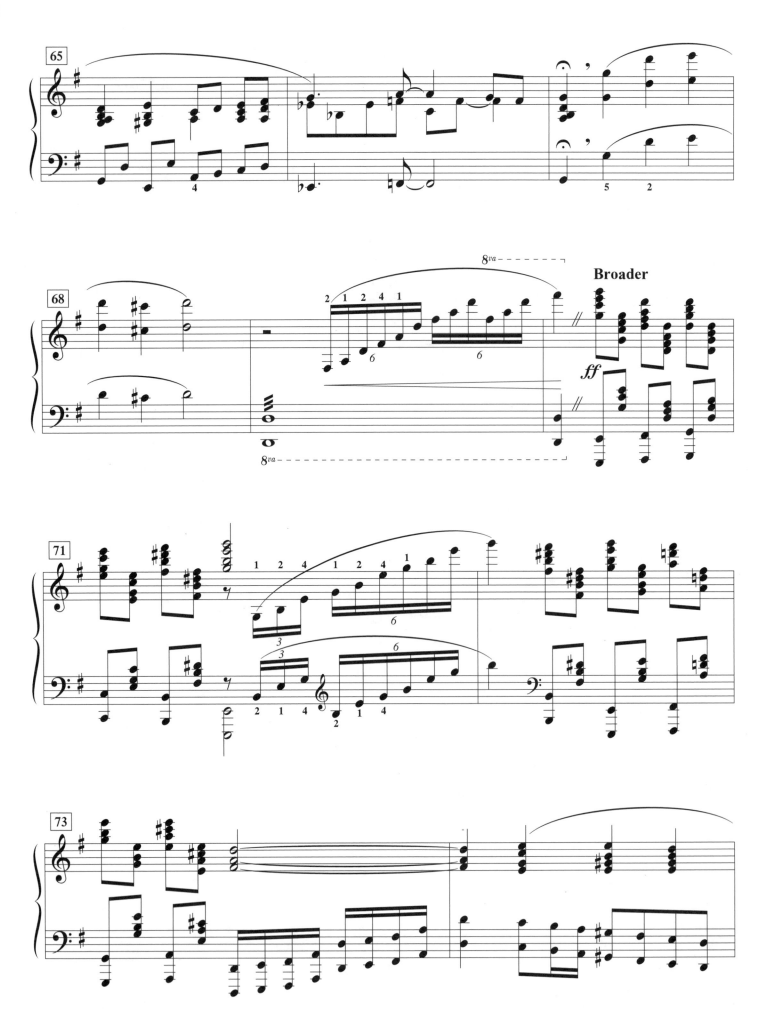

Turn Your Eyes upon Jesus
Lemmel

Helen H. Lemmel

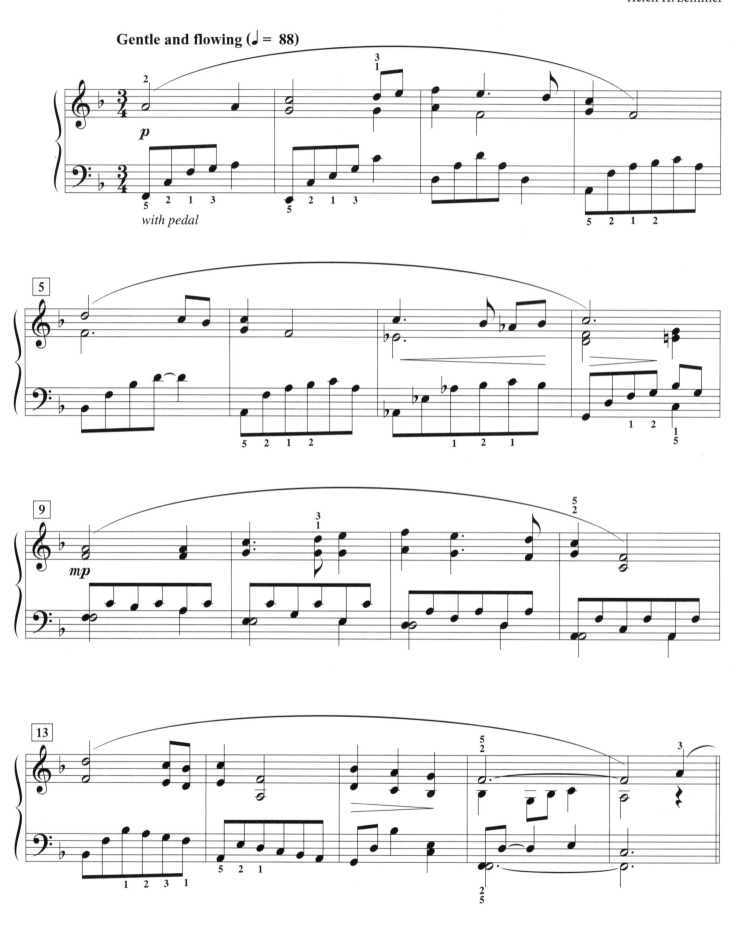

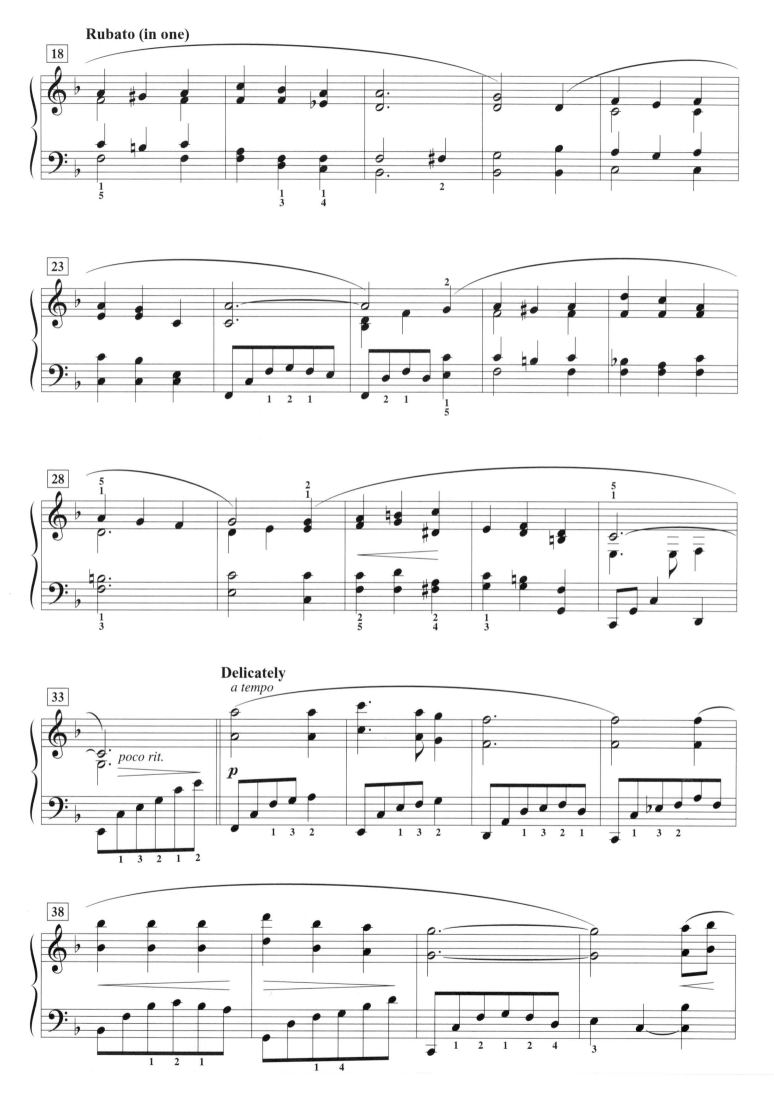

12

FF1393

Shout to the Lord

Shout to the Lord

Darlene Zschech

Very slowly, rubato, expressive

Jesus, the Very Thought of Thee

St. Agnes

John B. Dykes

Gentle and restful (♩ = ca. 80)

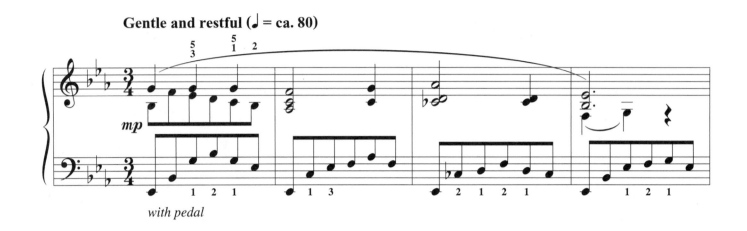

with pedal

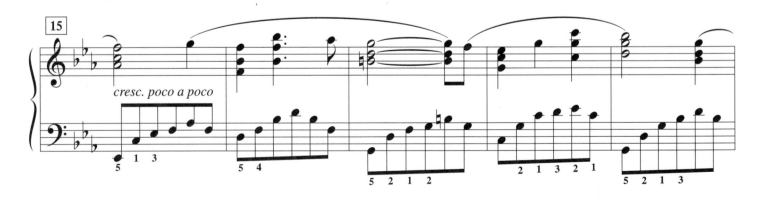

22

FF1393

We're Marching to Zion

Marching to Zion

Robert Lowry

FF1393

It Is Well with My Soul

Ville du Havre

Philip P. Bliss

Moving ahead (♩ = ca. 100)

Tempo primo (♩ = ca. 80)

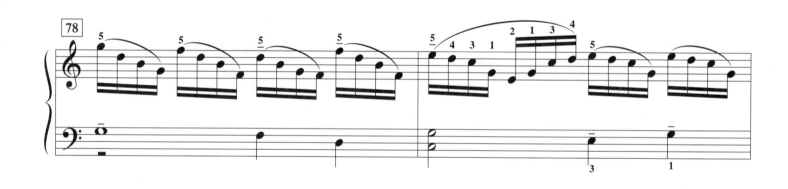

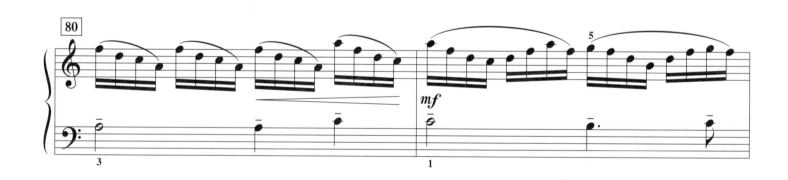

Faster, accented

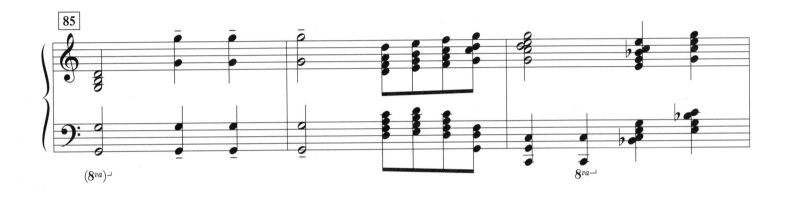

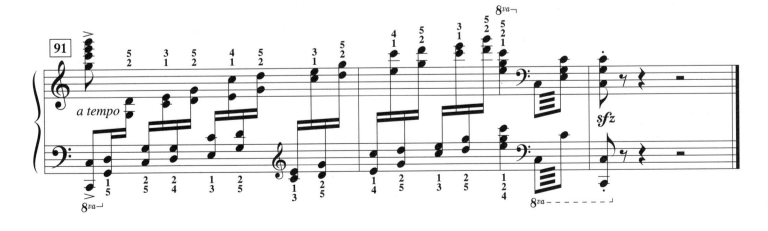

Rejoice, Ye Pure in Heart

Marion

Arthur H. Messiter

*Quoting the introduction to Chopin's Waltz in E Minor, Op. Post.

I Surrender All

Surrender

Winfield S. Weeden

Prayerfully and expressively ($\quarternote$ = ca. 69)

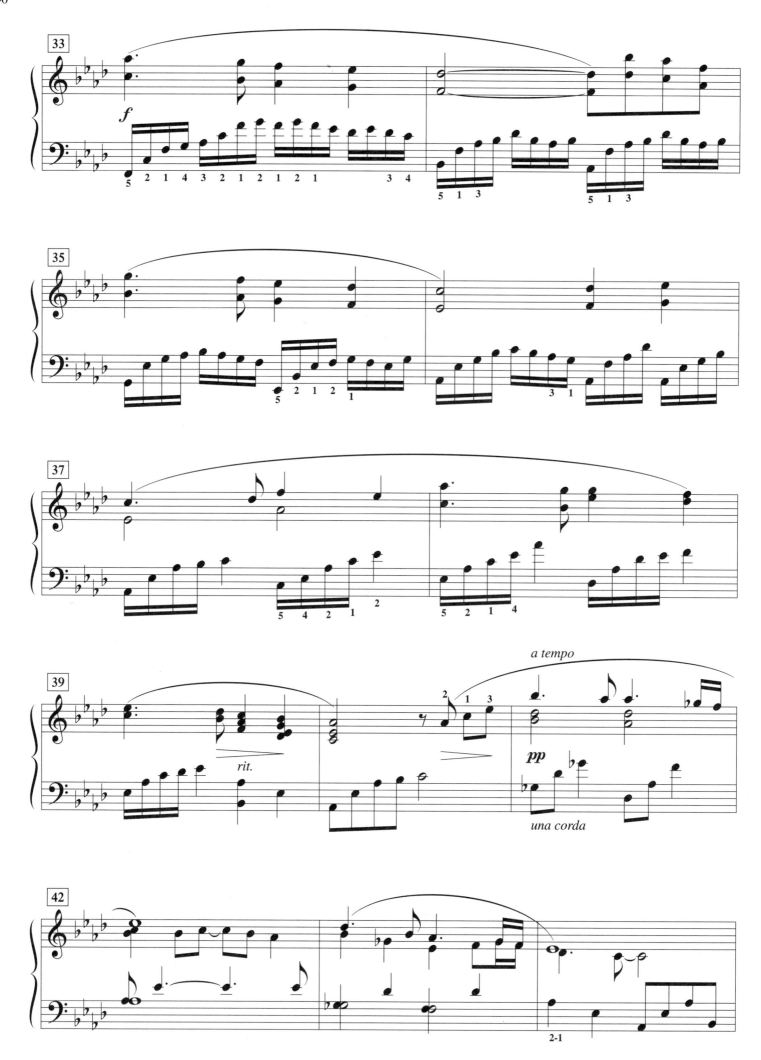

FF1393

Christ Arose

Christ Arose

Robert Lowry

This arrangement © 2003 The FJH Music Company Inc.

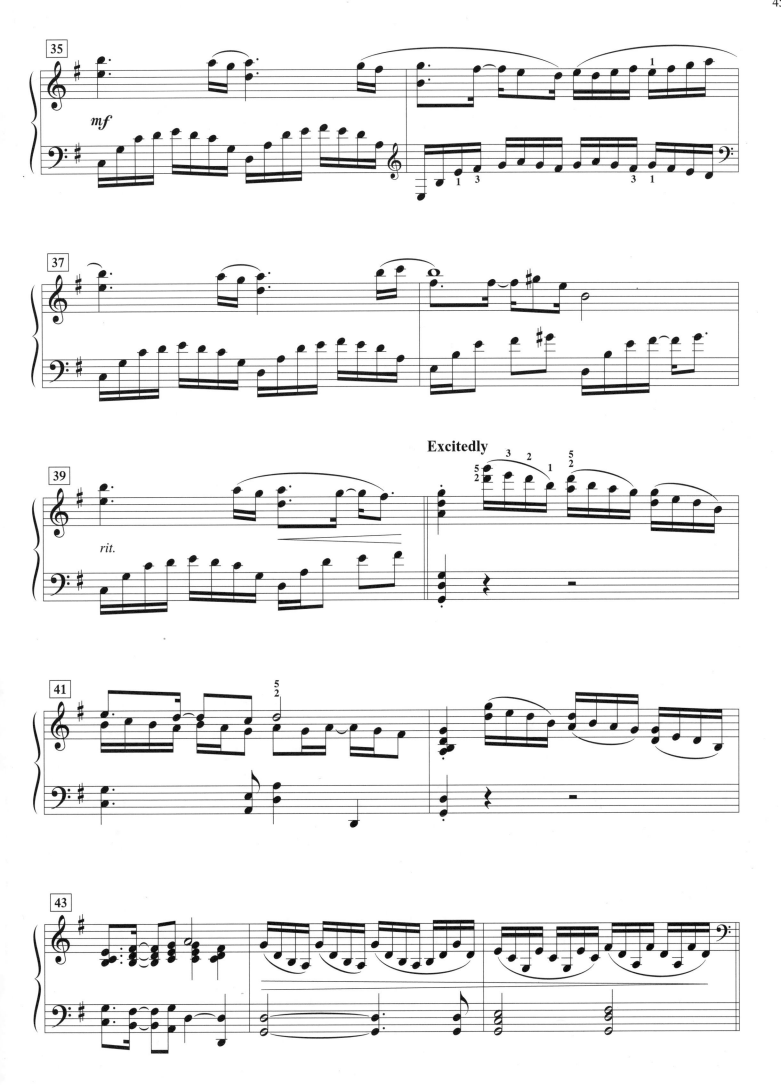

On Eagle's Wings

On Eagle's Wings

Michael Joncas

50

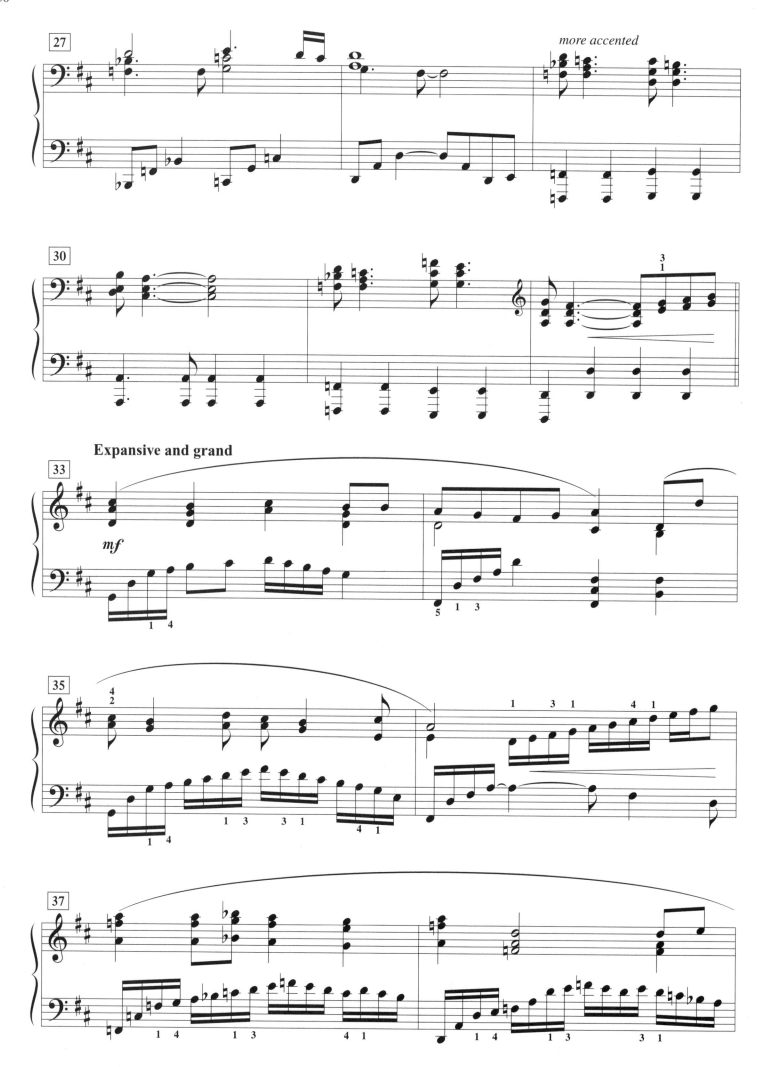

FF1393

Majestic and slower

52

A little faster

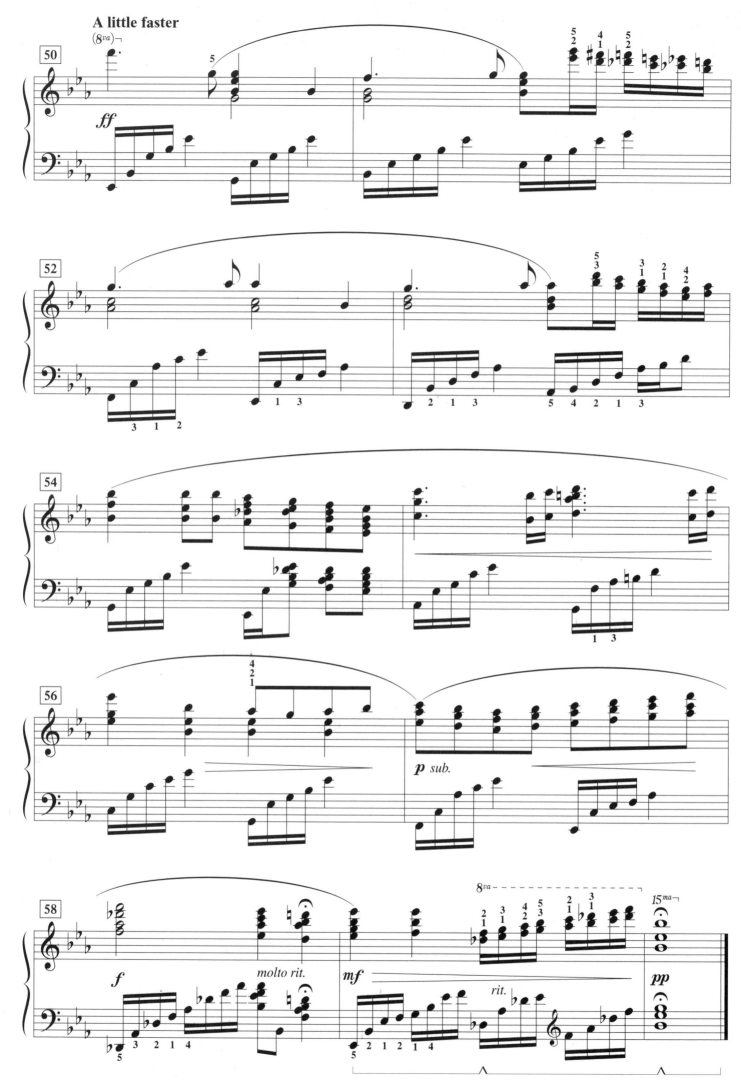